Plum Dreams Diary

On Mothers, Men, Modern Medicine, and the Divine

Joyce Lynn

Nancy —
Dream On!
Joyce Lynn

Plum Dreams Media

Plum Dreams Media
Dream Guidance for Positive Change
P.O. Box 682   Mill Valley, California 94942
415-267-7620   www.PlumDreams.com

ISBN 978-0-9834395-0-9

First Paperback Edition

Cover art and book design
Dandan Luo

Excerpt from *Gates of Prayer:*
The New Union Prayerbook
©1975 Central Conference of American Rabbis
reproduced by permission

To the Guide of Dreams
with immense gratitude

Dreams are the
language of the soul,
the voice of the Divine

CONTENTS

Prologue   5

TRUE SELF

Five Women Painting   11
Rescue   12
Drowning   14
If the Shoe Fits   15
Publish or Perish   17
Fear   18
Starfish   19

MOTHERS

Grandmother's Chair   23
From Sticker Lady   24
To Slicker Woman   25
Nearly New   26
Driven   27

MEN

Good-bye, Dolly   31
Push-ups   32
Party's Over   33
Super Men   34
Day Dreams   35
This Is It   36
Caring & Wise   37
Union Square   38

The Game 39
What a Racket 40
Make Love, Not War 41
No Parking 42

MODERN MEDICINE

Society Says 45
Pink Amaryllis 46
Consciousness Cure 47
Roots 48
Donut W/hole 49
Trivial Pursuits 50
Biblical Treatment 51
Inside 52
Words 53
Catch-22 54
Fields of Grain 55
MaxIwell 56
Fall of the Best Western 57

THE DIVINE

Guide of Dreams 61
Pillow Talk 62
Definitely Spiritual 63
Back to Art 64
Tiger in the Tank 65

AUTHOR'S NOTE:

PROLOGUE

Dreams bequeath sacred gifts. With wit and wisdom, these nocturnal visitors offer direction and guidance for our well-being.

I know this now, but for years I was a left-brained journalist, depending on rote and reason to navigate the world. An ambitious East Coast reporter, I covered politics in the nation's capital.

Although outwardly successful, I struggled with a phalanx of debilitating problems: writer's block, an acrimonious relationship with my mother, chronic health difficulties, failed romances, confused religious beliefs. And, this is only a partial list.

To overcome these impediments, I tried therapy, personal growth seminars, medical fixes, overeating — with mixed success.

In 1981, I moved to San Francisco, to the West Coast. Soon, a non-rational occurrence intruded. I remembered my first dream ever. It held contours of a crucial scene for the screenplay I was writing.

The dreams shared in *PLUM DREAMS DIARY* appeared on my night-time screen. Every morning, I recorded the scenes in a journal, playing with the symbols, images, and word puns. In this way, I taught myself to understand the dreams; in this way, the dreams taught me to integrate their lessons into my life.

We need more than intelligence and logical thinking to secure a meaningful life. Ancients and their spiritual traditions honored dreams as harbingers of healing the body and heart and of guiding a people. They revered the dream as sage wisdom.

Nightly encounters convinced me dreams are the language of the soul, the voice of the Divine.

Dreams continue to speak to me. I trust these messengers, calling upon their acumen.

During the potential health crisis retold in this book, the doctor said, probably to assuage my fears, "Well, for a writer these are important experiences." His comment made a dramatic impression.

The pioneering dreams in this book form a telling collection of choice dreams with the power to transform women's lives. This second edition reorders the remembrances into explorations of our true self, mothers, men, modern medicine, and the nature of the Divine.

As I update this Prologue, the guiding, prophetic, curative capacities of dreams are apparent. For compelling reasons, probe the dreams and contemplate their lessons for your life. For commanding insights, perceive the wealth your dreams hold.

We all carry the scars of growing up, disappointments in work and love, and fears about our health. We all want to find happiness and lead a meaningful life. May these pages inspire you to listen to dreams, imperative guideposts punctuating the way.

Joyce Lynn
Mill Valley, California, 2012

Grant, O Eternal God, that we may lie down in peace, and raise us up, O Sovereign, to life renewed. Spread over us the shelter of Your peace; guide us with Your good counsel; and for Your name's sake, be our Help.

— Gates of Prayer:
The New Union Prayerbook

So great a power is there of the soul upon the body that which ever way the soul imagines and dreams that it goes, doth it lead the body

— Agrippa,
16th century theologian and physician

TRUE SELF

FIVE WOMEN PAINTING

*A black and white etching of five women entwined
in work and play appears.*

The women pulsate with life.
In placid stillness,
moving effortlessly
combing hair
serenading
drawing
writing
reading

Whispering/singing/whistling.

Sunbursts, bold stripes, wavy lines
unfold horizontally.
Daisies mark the scene.

The women, different nationalities,
yet interrelated,
interconnected.

The women powerful simply because
they do not seek power.

They seek to empower themselves.
They seek to empower each other.

RESCUE

*People gather. An ambulance and police surround
a tree at Dominican College. I stand beside a bicycle.
Marriage prospects assemble here, too.*

The dream solves the plight of the plot of the
screenplay. Instead of struggling over every word,
I compose with ease.

At the altar, the heroine announces she is
disavowing her marriage.

JENNIFER

Since I was a
teenager, I've dreamt
every man I've dated
would save me from
singlehood, or I've done
it all myself.

I've pushed and pulled
men to love me — or
pretended it was no big deal.

Now, I'm giving up my search
for a rescuer and my fierce
struggle for independence.

Instead, the promise I'm
making today: I'm going
to find strength — real
strength — in myself.

The dream redirects the play — and its creator. Rather than manipulate external elements, like Jennifer, the writer contemplates turning inward to find the ineffable.

DROWNING

Flooding — the deluge of conformity — swirls outside an apartment building where people live apart.

A neighbor, the fearless expression of individuality, suggests a young woman, struggling to shatter the traditional female mold, take off her high heels.

Should she remove her shoes?

Wearing them, she stands tall, above the water. The young woman smiles and disappears.

Outside, a swirling torrent fills the back parking lot.

Leaving through the front door, I can walk to the car and avoid drowning.

IF THE SHOE FITS

A big stone mansion dominates the landscape at Yosemite National Park. Here, I wait for a high school friend.

Where is she?

Soon, she appears, prim and proper, wearing a tidy black dress and patented-leather heels, hair impeccably coiffed.

I hand her a pair of shoes from Chandler's or Baker's, the budget stores for confirmation, prom, and party pumps.

Lovely gowns, far more sophisticated than teenage yearnings, eclipsed the shoes: the strapless dress with wedding cake tiers, a midnight blue crinoline skirt embossed with violet lilies.

My cohort discards the shoes. "This is the second time a friend has returned my gift," I complain.

For years, attention fixed on the chintzy shoes diminished the alluring dresses. For decades, a down-at-the-heels image dominated retrospection.

The flourishing friend radiates only the best. Poised and assured, she picks me up.

Mr. Right-of-the-Moment appears and apologizes for acting like a slob. "You have another chance," I grant.

He wears elf shoes.

PUBLISH OR PERISH

Thinking — rather than picturing — what the screenplay co-writer once advised:

"Go through your resistance to success or go write commercials in Slippery Rock."

I repeat the axiom to another writer.

FEAR

Fear of failure.
    Fear of failing.

Only those words.

STARFISH

Pictures of camp friends appear.

A sun state beauty, curvy with flaming red locks;
another, lanky with mousy blonde hair.

Fast forward to the tall, athletic camper in her
thirties, wearing a color-coordinated suit, looking chic
and professional.

Then, back at camp, bunk mates have packed their
duffels. Did they find anything under their baggage?

The girls say fish — starfish.

As the camp director nurtured the talents and
abilities society and family squelch, under guidance of
the Divine, we can banish the insecurities accumulated
since childhood.

Then, we find our true Self.

Later, grown up, the lanky camper holds a
triangular piece of chocolate.

MOTHERS

GRANDMOTHER'S CHAIR

Mother dallies with my sisters. Now, it's too late.
Wellesley has accepted others. There is no place for me.
My sister stands before our grandmother's chair,
Rococo upholstered in silk brocade.
Aloud, I worry, "Someone could steal the chair."
Mother denies its worth; I insist on the significance.
A miniature china chair, adorned with her
grandmother's sepia picture, graces an antique curio.

What wild women! My mother, a take-no-prisoners
tennis player; my grandmother, a pioneer in a long
skirt on clay courts; my great grandmother, a foreign
correspondent for *The New York Times.*

The tableau evokes Judy Chicago's Dinner Party, an
artistic ode to women of legendary accomplishment.

The heroines speak. Instead of acquiescing to a
culture devaluing women, find value in yourself.

My grandmother's chair, covered in yellow, the
color of joy.

Joy, the root of Joyce, re-covers a sense of dignity.
Mother finally appreciates grandmother's chair.

FROM STICKER LADY

The founder of a popular toy company sits on the floor of her Victorian house. She copied a rival report.

A document prints before her paper.

Then, the toy maker and a woman with short-cropped hair celebrate the Sabbath together, eating pea soup.

How can they break bread after the businesswoman stole her plan?

The toy maker's account prints again.

Stickers, like lemons on the slot machines at Tahoe casinos, fill the document.

My report will not be child-like, infantile, but mature, for adults.

Petitioning a declaration we create a new relationship, I write Mother.

I want to feel authentic, not like a lemon, not like a slot machine, not labeled.

TO SLICKER WOMAN

Dressing for the rain, I don overalls like Sissy Spacek wore in The River.

The slicker protects from the flood of ugly words threatening to inundate mother and daughter.

I stuff the watch she gave me, her high school graduation present from my grandfather, inside my blouse to keep it dry, to protect my mother's gift.

She bequeathed life, she bestowed time.

Putting the watch next to my heart, I go outside.

NEARLY NEW

In the garage of my childhood home, clothes —
donations to the thrift store Mother managed as her
philanthropic contribution — fill three shopping carts.

She dispensed discarded items:
a white tennis skirt,
London Fog raincoat,
and sweater adorned with snowflakes.

Second-hand clothes,
second-hand rose.

Across the street, through a window,
a neighbor is typing, living in the present.

DRIVEN

Driving toward a dead-end street, Mother must turn right or left. She wants to turn left, so she moves into the arrow-marked lane.

Thinking she can turn with the traffic, she slides into the less crowded lane. But when she arrives at the end of the street, she can only turn right, taking us the wrong way.

Traveling at night to arrive at our destination, we follow a treacherous route through Sausalito — arriving at the Golden Gate Bridge. Mother could turn around and proceed to her destination, but she refuses.

Terror strikes the passengers. We wonder: Will we survive? One rider warns, "Going this way we have to cross the Cliffs of Dover."

The Cliffs, chalk white shores where embattled armies once clashed.

Finally, we arrive.

Like my mother, I am driving in the wrong direction.

A medical crisis — abnormal cells — forces confrontation with dominant patterns and fears and with the recognition a deep grasp of life is missing.

MEN

GOOD-BYE, DOLLY

The office mail clerk pushes a dolly cart outside City Hall.

I can return the cart before camping with the socially-conscious writer I have in mind for Mr. Right.
I can replace the cart used to deliver the mail;
I can scuttle the doll-like behavior engaged to deliver the male.

The Golden Gate bus stop in front of the restaurant Squids appears.

Squids, inky black sea creatures, armed with eight tentacles.
Eight, the number of death
and
regeneration.

PUSH-UPS

I am doing push-ups on a horizontal bar.

The message: Instead of pushing and pulling men, instead of coercing others, develop strength in your self.

I am somewhere with a dog, and the animal grows smaller.

PARTY'S OVER

In a motel room, Mr. Right-of-the-Moment stands by the window.

The Venetian blinds are drawn. I expect a celebration with champagne.

Instead, Styrofoam packing beads litter the floor.

SUPER MEN

The word processing supervisor approaches.
Like Superman, he wears a purple T-shirt.
He shifts into my father, who twists into
Mr. Right-of-the-Moment.

Word processing, turning words into story,
is my department.
So is spinning ordinary men into super men,
allowing their words, sharp as arrows, to pierce the soul.

The overseer wears a purple T-shirt.
Purple, the color of transformation.

DAY DREAMS

Wearing yellow-tinted sunglasses, seeing rainbows, I look out the window.

Mr. Right's daughter imitates, doing what I am doing.

Suddenly, she warns, "Step out of the street, so you're not blindsided."

THIS IS IT

The receptionist warns,
"You may not like it, but this is it."
She jumps up and down, pointing.
Mr. Right agrees, gesturing affirmatively.

I am not it.
Only the moment matters.

CARING & WISE

A man stands next to Karen Wise.

Does he accompany her because she is caring and wise — what men want, what we all want?

UNION SQUARE

The door from the parking garage to the Union Square hotel is locked.

A co-worker furnishes the key: a book about appreciating life titled Living, Loving and Learning.

The book opens the door.

As I descend on the escalator, a colleague and his girl friend, dressed in evening clothes, ride up the other side.

The ballroom turns into my wedding reception. A high school classmate, a computer software specialist wearing a fancy tuxedo, appears.

Will he give me the program for achieving happiness in relationships like the intimate couple in night wear?

Later, he ascends on the escalator at the Civic Center subway station.

The question in the parking lot: Can rearranging external circumstances construct an elusive balance?

The answer: Loving relationships and humane work emanate from the center of our being, from within.

THE GAME

From my hand/first-hand,

I recognize a long-time fear —
    winning at work
        will cost in love.

Afraid
    if I play the ace,
        I will lose the game.

WHAT A RACKET

Mr. Right-of-the-Moment talks on the telephone, trying to reach a woman. He writes a message and signs it "Simpson."

Why does he act with duplicity?

....

On an airplane with two men, I give each a different racket.

One is metal, one is wood — like my two tennis rackets.

MAKE LOVE, NOT WAR

A faded red MG, like our friend drove when my lawfully-wedded husband abandoned me for her, rolls in front of my car.

The vehicle ahead of mine stops the sports car — just as my next romantic liaison deadened the pain of a splintered marriage.

Around the corner, a car catches fire. Someone pours out the gasoline.

A robber breaks into a windowless rec shelter. I call for help, escaping while others tarry.

On the beach, a child plays.

A yellow-white flash of light, like nuclear war, fills the sky.

When friends make love with friends' lovers, they make war with friends.

War scares kids.

NO PARKING

Tonight, a date with a new love interest. He is
short, pugnacious, reeling from a painful divorce.

*A bulldog and a red line painted on the curb in
front of my apartment appear on my dream screen.*

The warning signals impinge on the thrill
of romance.
The conflict endures between pre-determinism
and free will, between guidance and disobedience.
The debate about our will and God's will is no longer
an existential exercise.
Experientially, I know: We choose what will
bring disaster or delight.

MODERN MEDICINE

SOCIETY SAYS

Riding in a bus to my former gynecologist's office,
I sit in the handicapped section.
The driver says disparagingly,"Ugh, you're disgusting.
Around your mouth is dirty, and you have lesions on
your skin."

The man driving the bus — Society — berates
women who speak out.

The next day the doctor calls, announcing an
abnormal Pap test result.

The dream, an internal female exam, reveals
embodied cultural condemnation.

Even though I renounced hurts from sullied
romantic relationships, I still harbor indelible wounds.

People donning B.U.M. Equipment sweatshirts
literally wear their attitudes on their sleeves. I carry
mine inside.

I play leapfrog with Mr. Right-of-the-Moment.
Squatting like a frog, he waits for me.
Then, he leaps over my back, a prophecy of my fate
with an imaginary prince.

PINK AMARYLLIS

In a newsroom, no, it's a bank, desks fill the
loan section.
Co-workers gather, napping rather than
reading newspapers.
"I'll go to sleep, too," I say.
Frida is here. An amaryllis adorns her desk.
The beautiful, open flower is pink.
Shocking pink. Vibrant pink.
Now sitting on my left hand,
I admire the pink flower,

a delicate reminder of desired mending and
emotional flowering.

CONSCIOUSNESS CURE

Fear about the abnormal cells plagues me.

*I wake up in an operating room. No, the space
is a kitchen. I put a big wire whisk in the center of a
silver flower. Now, the object is a cookie cutter, a metal
container.*

I am cutting out unwanted images from memory,
from the past.

ROOTS

I live on an island.
It is the house where I grew up.
Gold sconces on the hallway wall contain the source
of health maladies.

The planters hold the seeds of my belief society
disparages women desiring a happy family life and a
successful career.

DONUT W/HOLE

Donuts fill two glass plates on a cafe table: one donut with a hole; the other, dusted with powdered sugar, solid.

Like a beignet from the French Quarter in New Orleans, the solid donut looks normal.

I choose the whole donut, not the donut with the hole.

I choose wholeness.

TRIVIAL PURSUITS

Someone asks, "What color is Manhattan clam chowder, red or white?"

Why, I wonder, do we waste time in trivial pursuits?

BIBLICAL TREATMENT

A tent preacher performs a miracle on a blind man.
His powers impress me, and I want him to heal me.
Holding down the preacher, I persevere until he
performs a miracle on me.

Through the Biblical-like cure, abnormal cells in the nub of womanhood disappear.

INSIDE

A shadowy figure climbs the flight of stairs, kicks aside a brightly colored toy train so no one will trip.
The train bangs against a wall.
The phantasm enters a house and a small area, looks at the pure, impressionable baby in a crib, and raises the side to protect the child.

(Inserting interpretations) conjures a healing formula:
Change the train of thought
dominating your life,
    change your behavior,
    activate the deep, loving part of
        the Self
            and
                find your self.

(Or, perhaps, activate the deep, loving part of your self and find the Self)

WORDS

In the dream, a voice speaks enigmatic words:

"We don't have very much caring in California, do we?"

CATCH-22

A board game, like Concentration or Memory, is missing. A college roommate asks the location.

In the closet, perhaps.

A box called Time or Monopoly fills the shelf.

The top is open.

Since college, a game of self-defeating thoughts and attitudes derailed desires and abilities.

The game is over, and a Catch-22 ensues, a gap between what existed and the experience of what existed.

An opportunity looms to explore life, create a relationship with the Self, and encounter deep-seated feelings and hidden ideas.

In mind contests, the imagination holds the power of change.

TIME is the name of the game,
and the lid is off.

FIELDS OF GRAIN

What will lead to healthy living?

A sheaf of wheat blowing in the wind appears on my dream screen.

The same design decorates a flyer for a vegetarian cooking class, signaling the way.

Its bedrock, the Eating Plan from the Garden of Eden, prescribed in the Bible.

MAXIWELL

The word MAXIWELL.

MaxIwell,
  a mantra-in-the-making:
I maximize well-being.
I maximize my well-being.
I maximize well-being.
The soundings of a primordial secret:
  The potential to heal dwells within.

FALL OF THE BEST WESTERN

A Best Western motel collapses.

Is this the fall of Western medicine?

I feel the power of dreams and imagine health care unlike modern medicine.

Now, I wonder: Can frames of mind cause and cure illness?

The premise of the night time apparition:

Thoughts, attitudes, and beliefs — images appropriated from family and society — affect well-being.

Changing the image can change our life.

THE DIVINE

GUIDE OF DREAMS

The gourmet chef recommends Mitzi, a cooking
shop proprietor.
    Her location is near a square or park.
    "Oh, MacArthur Park perhaps?"
    "No," she responds," further over."
    Toward the financial district, near the center, near
the heart of the city?
    "Yes," she says. "It's inconvenient from the north, but
accessible from the east."

    East, Eastern, the hallowed sector.
    Mitzi, from mitt, a form of protection.
    Mitzi, from the Hebrew mitzvot, good deeds
linking the physical and the sacred.
    Mitzi, the Divine Spirit in every soul.

PILLOW TALK

A dark-haired, handsome man, dressed like a soldier, lies on the floor, kissing a blonde-haired woman.

The scene resembles Rock Hudson and Doris Day in an old-time movie.

DEFINITELY SPIRITUAL

A pair of Oriental slippers, the black variety from Chinatown, covers feet clothed in bright blue iridescent socks.

BACK TO ART

She warns,"No more gross men. I'm going back
to Art."

With her husband Art, she acts herself.
She says "I," but she counsels:
Abandon the senseless (bulldog) relationship and
return to Art,
    your true Self.

TIGER IN THE TANK

At the Tam Junction Arco station, a tiger fills up the gas tank.

Now, the tiger fills the tank.

In Chinese horoscopes, in Eastern lore, the tiger protects life.

The tiger resides inside.

OWED TO DREAMS

Dreams, a wellspring of creativity,

a reservoir of ideas.

Wisdom flows from an Inner Source,

revealing endless answers

to waking quandaries and questions.

Where fear once ruled,

confidence reigns.

ABOUT THE AUTHOR

Joyce Lynn is a journalist, speaker, and advocate for the empowerment of women.

After eight years as a political reporter in Washington, D.C., Joyce moved to San Francisco, where she recalled her first dream, ever. It redirected her path toward helping women use dreams for well-being.

When Joyce faced a health crisis, dreams were the place where healing happened. Dreams continue to guide all aspects of her life.

She is founder and editor of the online publications, *Political Diary, Plum Dreams Journal,* and *IS,* integrating information, intuition, and imagination for positive change. Her incisive stories and profiles help readers learn the truth of an issue. As a result, hers is a voice seldom heard in the media.

Joyce holds a Bachelor's degree in education and a Master's degree in communication. She was an assistant press secretary to a U.S. Representative and editor of a weekly newspaper.

Her mission: to share the power of dreams for our personal and social transformation.

Made in the USA
Charleston, SC
05 January 2013